THE GREATEST SHOWMAN

ORIGINAL SONGS BY
BENJ PASEK & JUSTIN PAUL

ISBN 978-1-5400-3797-8

E-Z Play Today® Music Notation © 1975 by Hal Leonard Corporation
E-Z PLAY and EASY ELECTRONIC KEYBOARD MUSIC are registered trademarks of Hal Leonard Corporation.

Visit Hal Leonard Online at
www.halleonard.com

Contact Us:
Hal Leonard
7777 West Bluemound Road
Milwaukee, WI 53213
Email: info@halleonard.com

In Europe contact:
Hal Leonard Europe Limited
42 Wigmore Street
Marylebone, London, W1U 2RN
Email: info@halleonardeurope.com

In Australia contact:
Hal Leonard Australia Pty. Ltd.
4 Lentara Court
Cheltenham, Victoria, 3192 Australia
Email: info@halleonard.com.au

FINGERING CHART

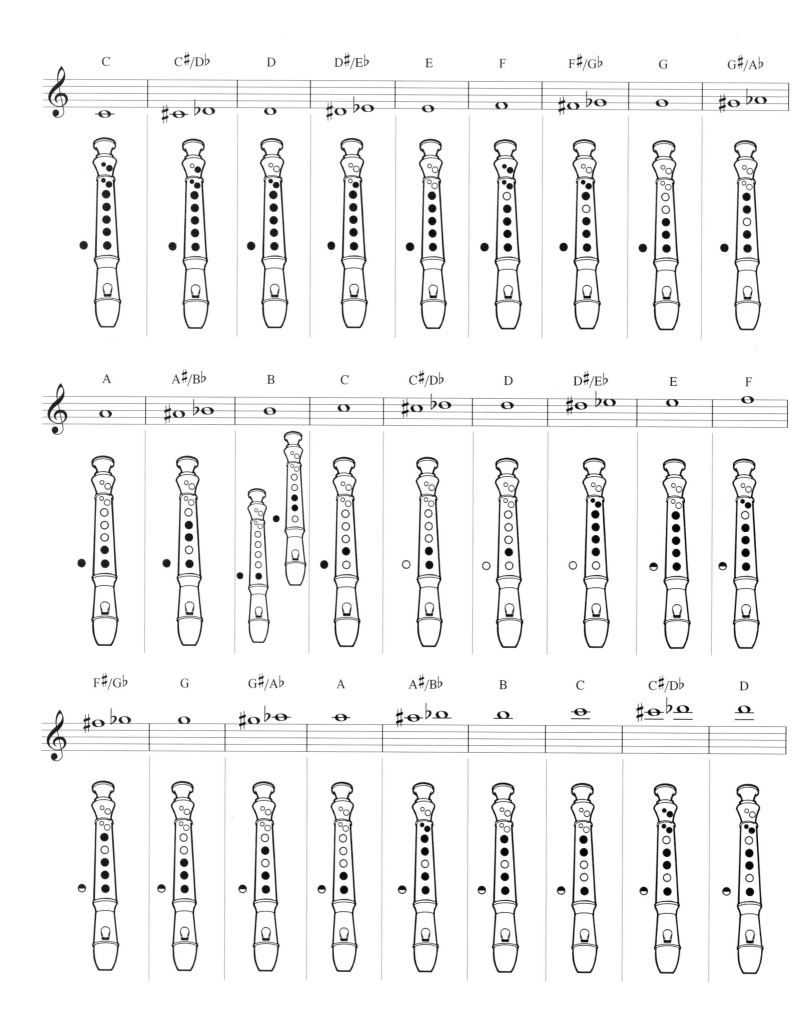

CONTENTS

SONGS

GETTING STARTED

HOLDING THE RECORDER

Here is how to hold the recorder. The mouthpiece rests on your lower lip, just like a drinking straw, with only a little of it actually going inside your mouth. Be sure that all of the finger holes line up on the front of the recorder as shown in the picture.

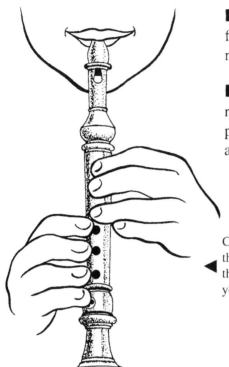

LEFT HAND — The first three fingers of your left hand (the little finger is not used) play the *top* three holes on the front of the recorder. The thumb of your left hand plays the hole on the back.

RIGHT HAND — The *bottom* four holes are played by your right-hand fingers. There is no hole for your right-hand thumb to play so it can help hold the recorder steady while the other fingers are busy playing.

◄ Cover the top three holes with your left-hand fingers and the bottom four holes with your right-hand fingers. The thumb of your left hand covers the hole in the back of your recorder.

MAKING A SOUND

To make a sound on the recorder blow gently into the small opening at the top of the mouthpiece. You can change this sound by covering different holes with your thumb and fingers. For example, when you cover all of the thumb and finger holes you will get a low, quiet sound. When only one or two holes are covered the sound will be higher and much louder.

Here are some tips for getting the best possible sound out of your recorder:

Always blow gently into the mouthpiece — Breathe in and then gently blow into the mouthpiece as if you were sighing or using a straw to blow out a candle. Remember, always blow gently.

Leaks cause squeaks — Play the holes using the pads of your fingers and thumb (not the tips). Press against each hole firmly so that it is completely covered and no air can sneak out. Even a tiny leak of air will change a beautiful tone into a sudden squeak!

Use your tongue to start each tone — Place your tongue against the roof of your mouth just behind your front teeth and start each tone that you play by tonguing the syllable "du" or "too" as you blow gently into the recorder.

PLAYING A TONE

Musical sounds are called *tones*. Every tone has a letter name. *Finger charts* are used to show you exactly which holes should be covered in order to play a particular tone. Each circle on these charts represents one of the holes on your recorder. The thumb hole is represented by the circle to the left of the recorder in the chart.

●   means that you should cover that hole.

○   means that that hole should not be covered but left open.

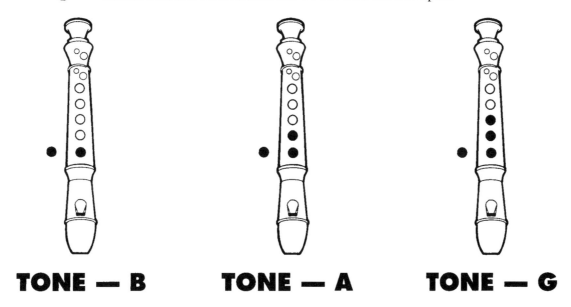

TONE — B   **TONE — A**   **TONE — G**

Use these three tones to play "Mary Had A Little Lamb:"

MARY HAD A LITTLE LAMB

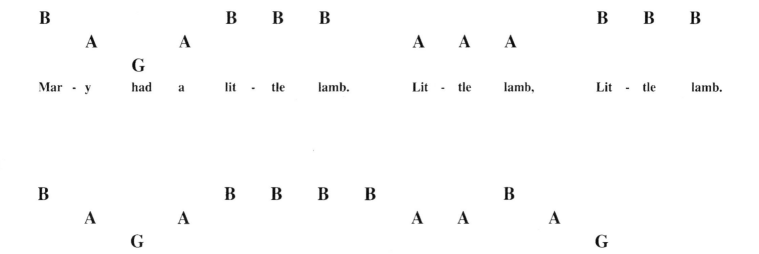

READING MUSIC

Musical notes are an easy way to see everything that you need to know in order to play a song on your recorder:

How high or low — Notes are written on five lines that are called a *staff*. The higher a note is written on the staff the higher it will sound.

How long or short — The color of a note (black or white) tells you if it should be played short or long. The black notes in "Mary Had A Little Lamb" are all one beat long (*quarter notes*). The first three white notes in this song are two beats long (*half notes*) and the last note is four beats long (*whole note*).

How the beats are grouped — The two numbers at the beginning of the song (4/4) are called a *time signature*. This time signature tells you that the *beats* in this song are grouped in fours: **1** 2 3 4 **1** 2 3 4 etc. To help you see this grouping, *bar lines* are drawn across the staff to mark each *measure* of four beats. A *double bar* is used to mark the end of the song.

Now here is how "Mary Had A Little Lamb" looks when it is written in musical notes:

MARY HAD A LITTLE LAMB

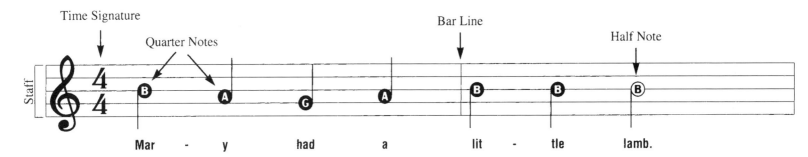

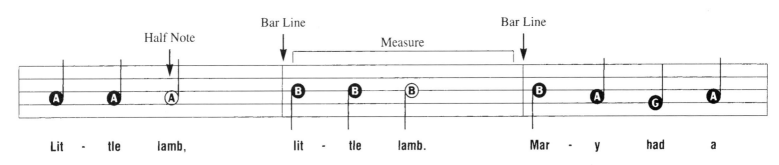

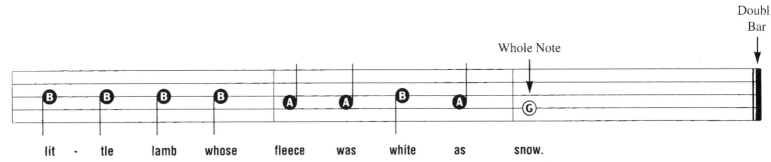

TWO NEW TONES

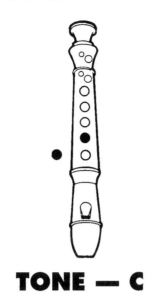

TONE — C

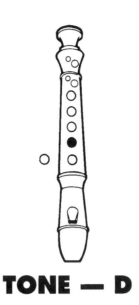

TONE — D

AURA LEE

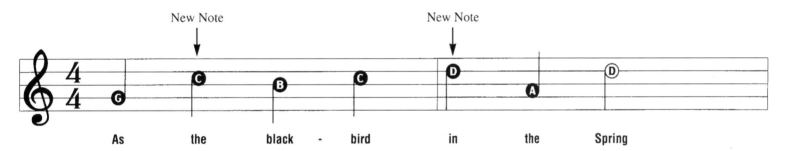

New Note   New Note

G   C   B   C   D   A   D

As   the   black - bird   in   the   Spring

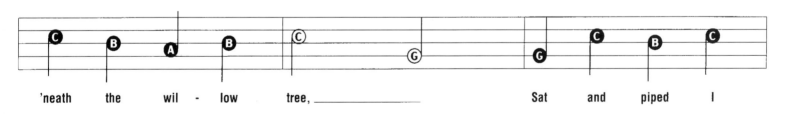

C   B   A   B   C   G   G   C   B   C

'neath   the   wil - low   tree, _____   Sat   and   piped   I

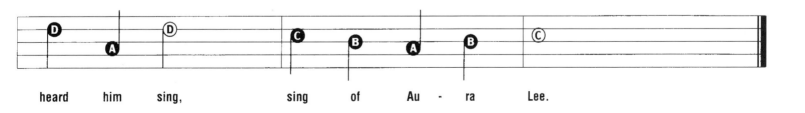

D   A   D   C   B   A   B   C

heard   him   sing,   sing   of   Au - ra   Lee.

USING YOUR RIGHT HAND

"Twinkle, Twinkle Little Star" uses the tone E. As you can see from the fingering chart, you will use three fingers of your left hand and two fingers of your right to play this tone. The thumb hole is only half filled in (◐). This means that you should "pinch" the hole with your thumb so that only a small part of the hole is left open. Pinching is done by bending your thumb so that the thumbnail points directly into the recorder leaving the top of the thumb hole open.

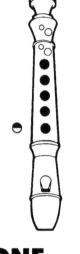

TONE — E

TWINKLE, TWINKLE LITTLE STAR

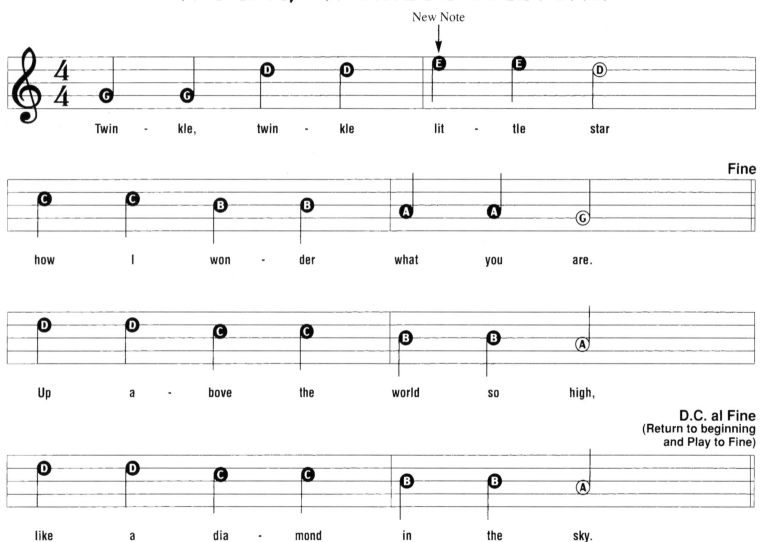

Copyright © 1992 by HAL LEONARD PUBLISHING CORPORATION
International Copyright Secured   All Rights Reserved

NOTES AND RESTS

In addition to notes that are one, two or four beats long, other values are possible. Also, *rests* are used to indicate when you should *not* play a tone but be silent. The chart on page 7 will help you identify the different notes and rests that are used in this book.

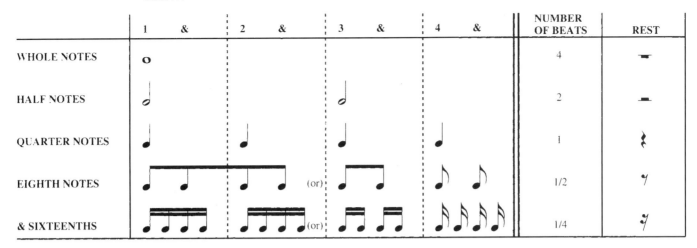

	COUNT: 1 & 2 & 3 & 4 &	NUMBER OF BEATS	REST
WHOLE NOTES		4	
HALF NOTES		2	
QUARTER NOTES		1	
EIGHTH NOTES	(or)	1/2	
& SIXTEENTHS	(or)	1/4	

DOTTED NOTES ARE 1 1/2 TIMES THE NORMAL LENGTH:

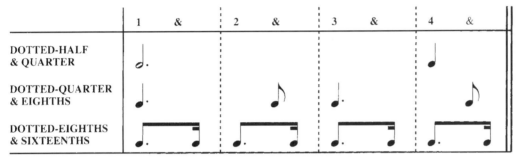

	1 & 2 & 3 & 4 &
DOTTED-HALF & QUARTER	
DOTTED-QUARTER & EIGHTHS	
DOTTED-EIGHTHS & SIXTEENTHS	

TRIPLETS ARE SPREAD EVENLY ACROSS THE BEATS:

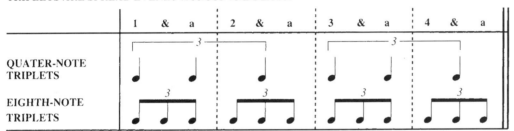

	1 & a 2 & a 3 & a 4 & a
QUATER-NOTE TRIPLETS	
EIGHTH-NOTE TRIPLETS	

THIS OLD MAN

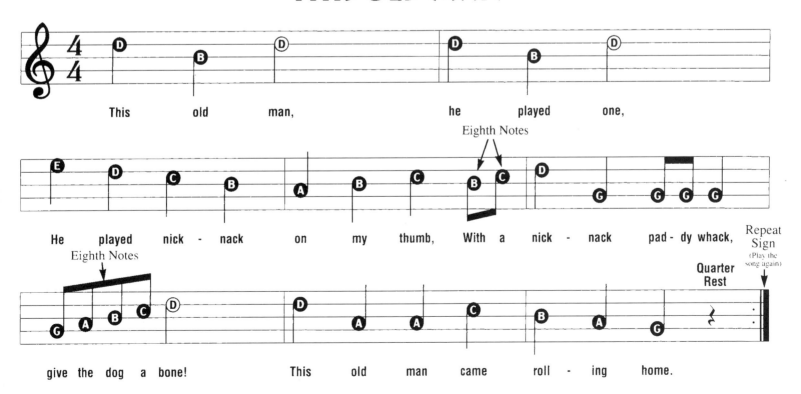

This old man, he played one,

Eighth Notes

He played nick - nack on my thumb, With a nick - nack pad - dy whack,

Eighth Notes

Quarter Rest

Repeat Sign (Play the song again)

give the dog a bone! This old man came roll - ing home.

THE GREATEST SHOW

Words and Music by Benj Pasek,
Justin Paul and Ryan Lewis

A MILLION DREAMS

Words and Music by Benj Pasek
and Justin Paul

COME ALIVE

Words and Music by Benj Pasek
and Justin Paul

Barnum: Come a - live, _____ come a - live _____

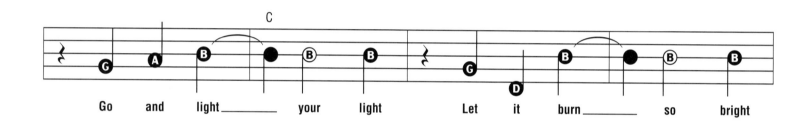

Go and light _____ your light Let it burn _____ so bright

Reach - in' up _____ to the sky, _____

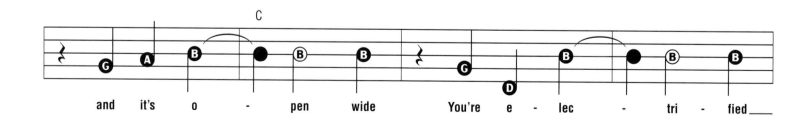

and it's o - pen wide You're e - lec - tri - fied ____

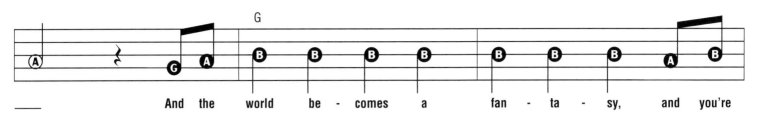

And the world be - comes a fan - ta - sy, and you're

more than you could ev - er be, 'cause you're dream - in' with your eyes___ wide

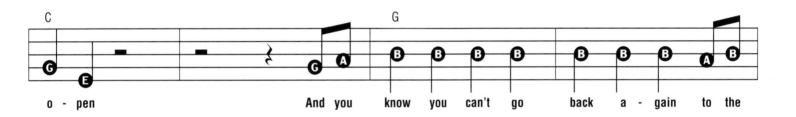

o - pen   And you know you can't go back a - gain to the

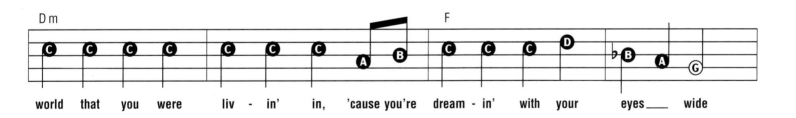

world that you were liv - in' in, 'cause you're dream - in' with your eyes___ wide

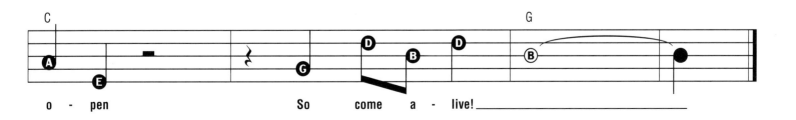

o - pen   So come a - live!_____

THE OTHER SIDE

Words and Music by Benj Pasek
and Justin Paul

REWRITE THE STARS

Words and Music by Benj Pasek
and Justin Paul

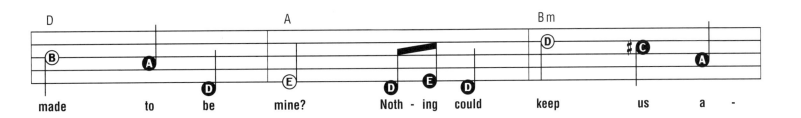

Phillip: What if we re - write the stars? Say you were

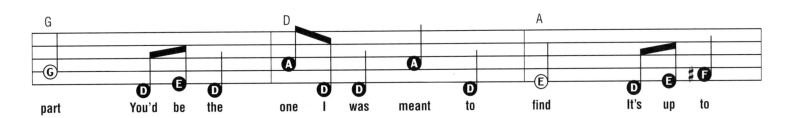

made to be mine? Noth - ing could keep us a -

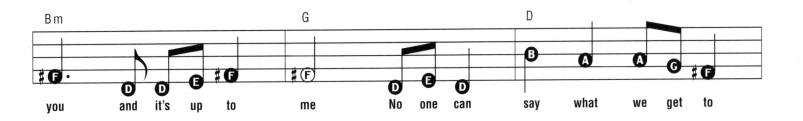

part You'd be the one I was meant to find It's up to

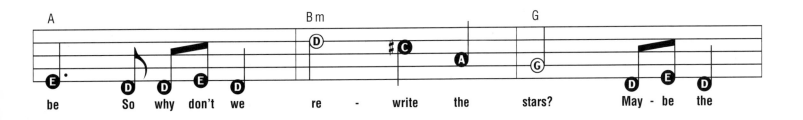

you and it's up to me No one can say what we get to

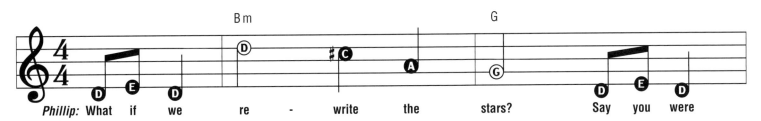

be So why don't we re - write the stars? May - be the

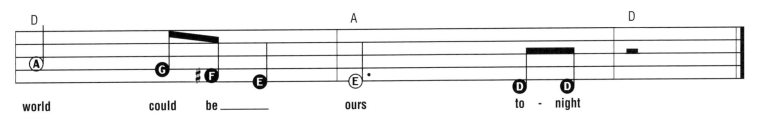

world could be _____ ours to - night

NEVER ENOUGH

Words and Music by Benj Pasek
and Justin Paul

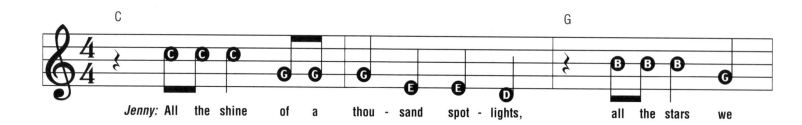

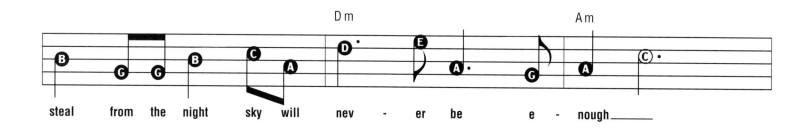

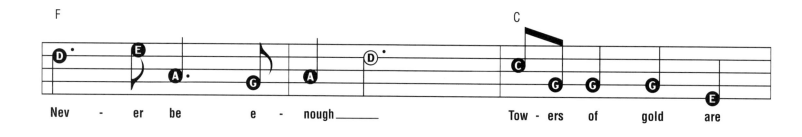

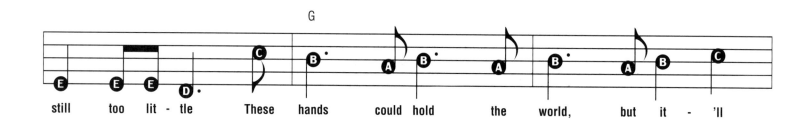

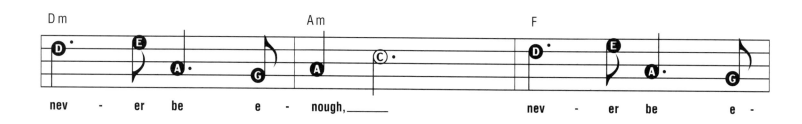

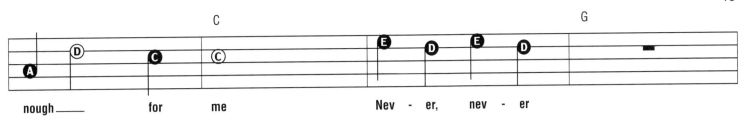

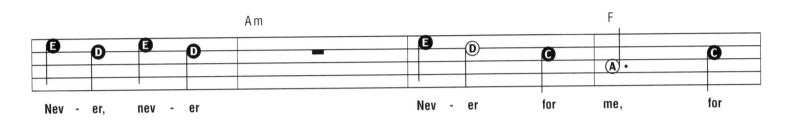

Nev - er, nev - er   Nev - er   for   me,   for

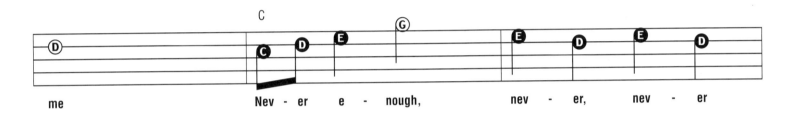

me   Nev - er e - nough,   nev - er,   nev - er

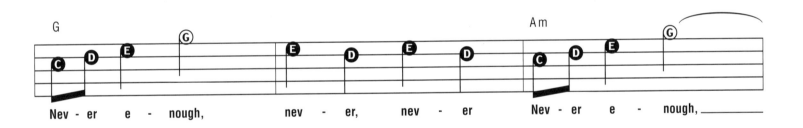

Nev - er e - nough,   nev - er,   nev - er   Nev - er e - nough, _____

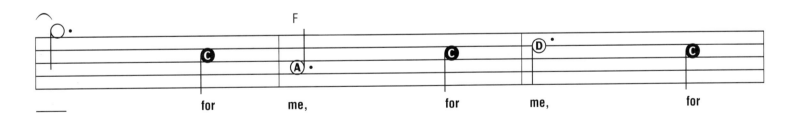

_____   for   me,   for   me,   for

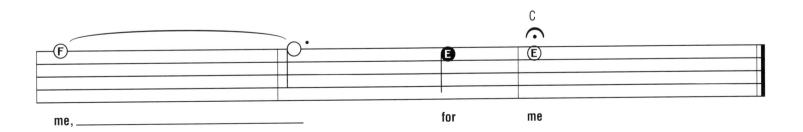

me, _____   for   me

THIS IS ME

Words and Music by Benj Pasek
and Justin Paul

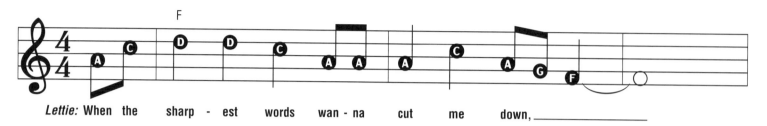

Lettie: When the sharp - est words wan - na cut me down, _____

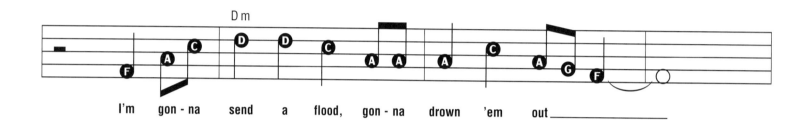

I'm gon - na send a flood, gon - na drown 'em out _____

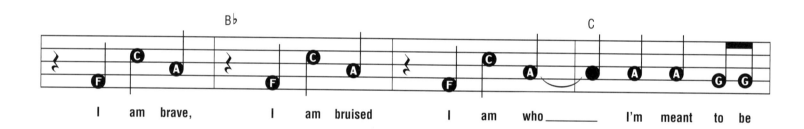

I am brave, I am bruised I am who _____ I'm meant to be

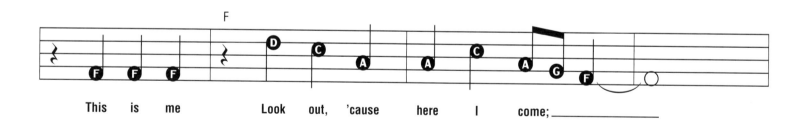

This is me Look out, 'cause here I come; _____

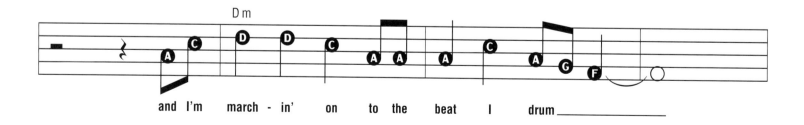

and I'm march - in' on to the beat I drum _____

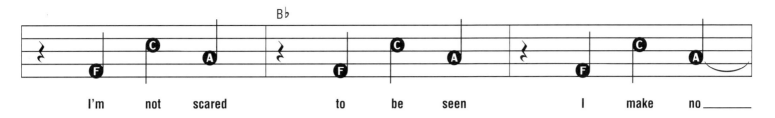

I'm not scared to be seen I make no

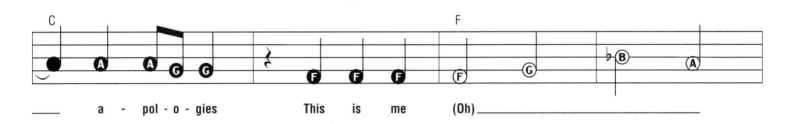

a - pol - o - gies This is me (Oh)

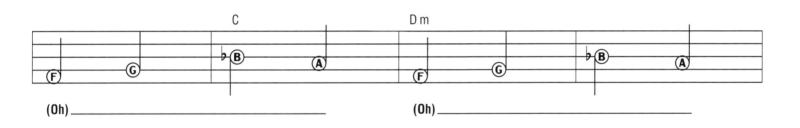

(Oh) (Oh)

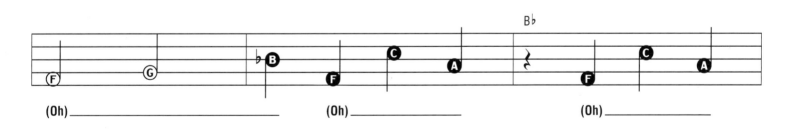

(Oh) (Oh) (Oh)

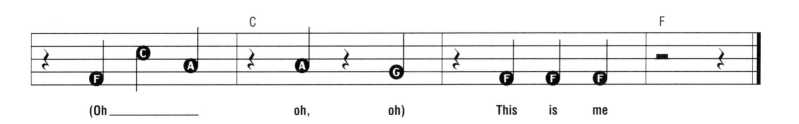

(Oh oh, oh) This is me

TIGHTROPE

Words and Music by Benj Pasek
and Justin Paul

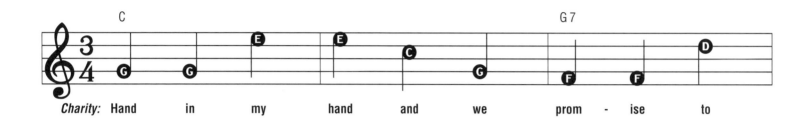

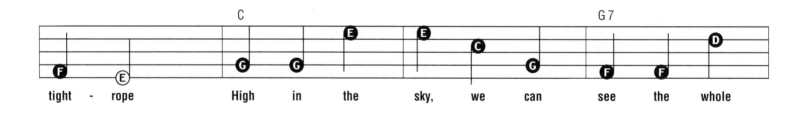

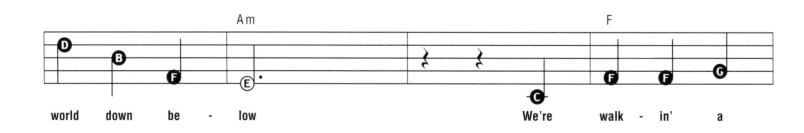

tight - rope _____ Nev - er sure,

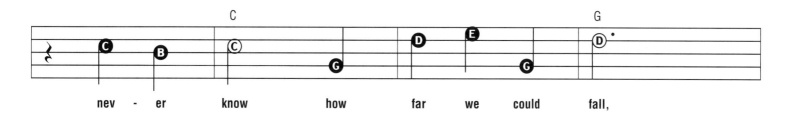

nev - er know how far we could fall,

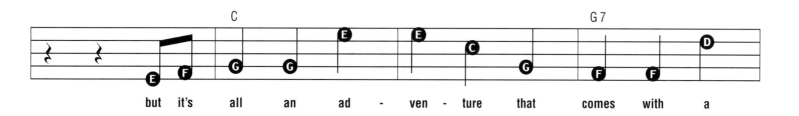

but it's all an ad - ven - ture that comes with a

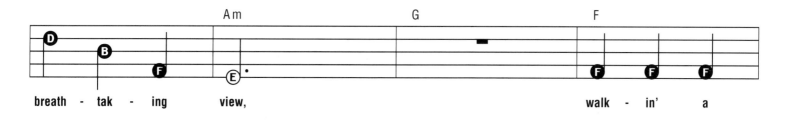

breath - tak - ing view, walk - in' a

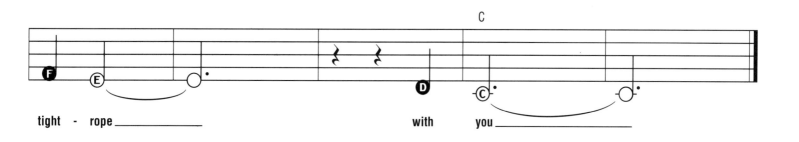

tight - rope _____ with you _____

FROM NOW ON

Words and Music by Benj Pasek
and Justin Paul